Skeletunes

Read along or sing to the tune of "Jingle Bells"

Julie Kirsch Akers

Copyright © 2024 Julie Kirsch Akers
All rights reserved
First Edition

PAGE PUBLISHING
Conneaut Lake, PA

First originally published by Page Publishing 2024

ISBN 979-8-89157-857-9 (pbk)
ISBN 979-8-89157-896-8 (hc)
ISBN 979-8-89157-858-6 (digital)

Printed in the United States of America

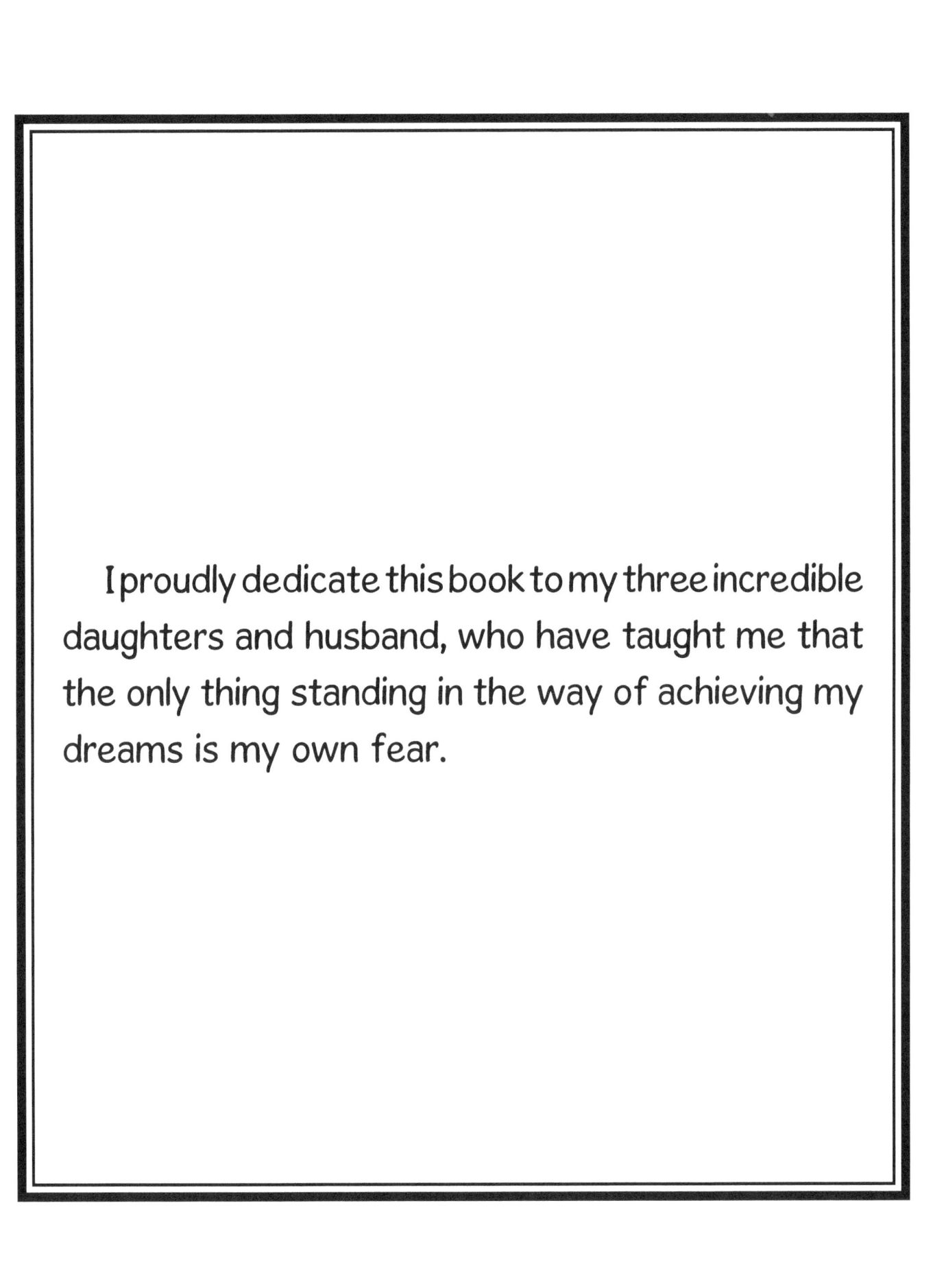

I proudly dedicate this book to my three incredible daughters and husband, who have taught me that the only thing standing in the way of achieving my dreams is my own fear.

The **CRANIUM** protects the brain,
And is otherwise known as the skull.

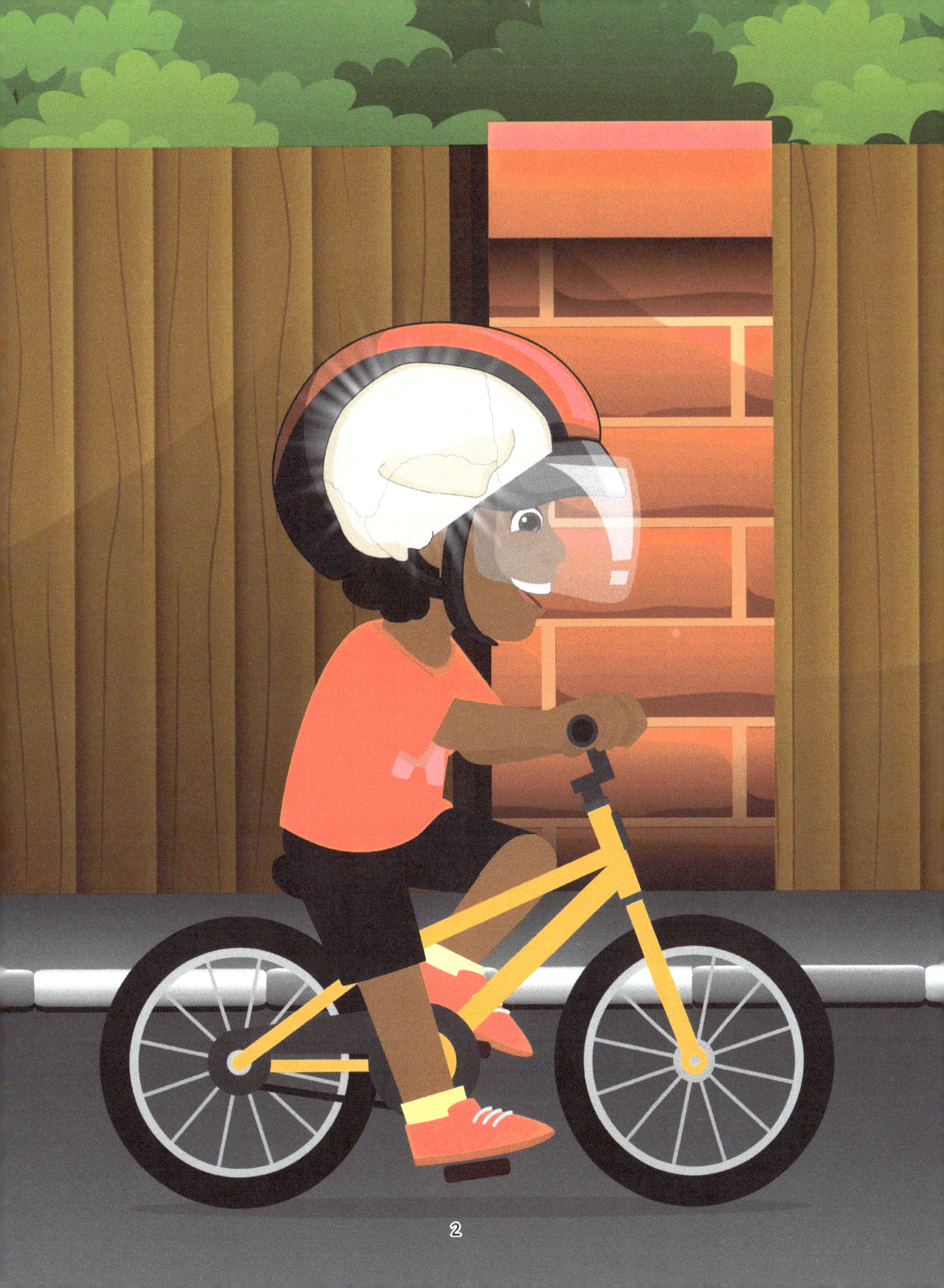

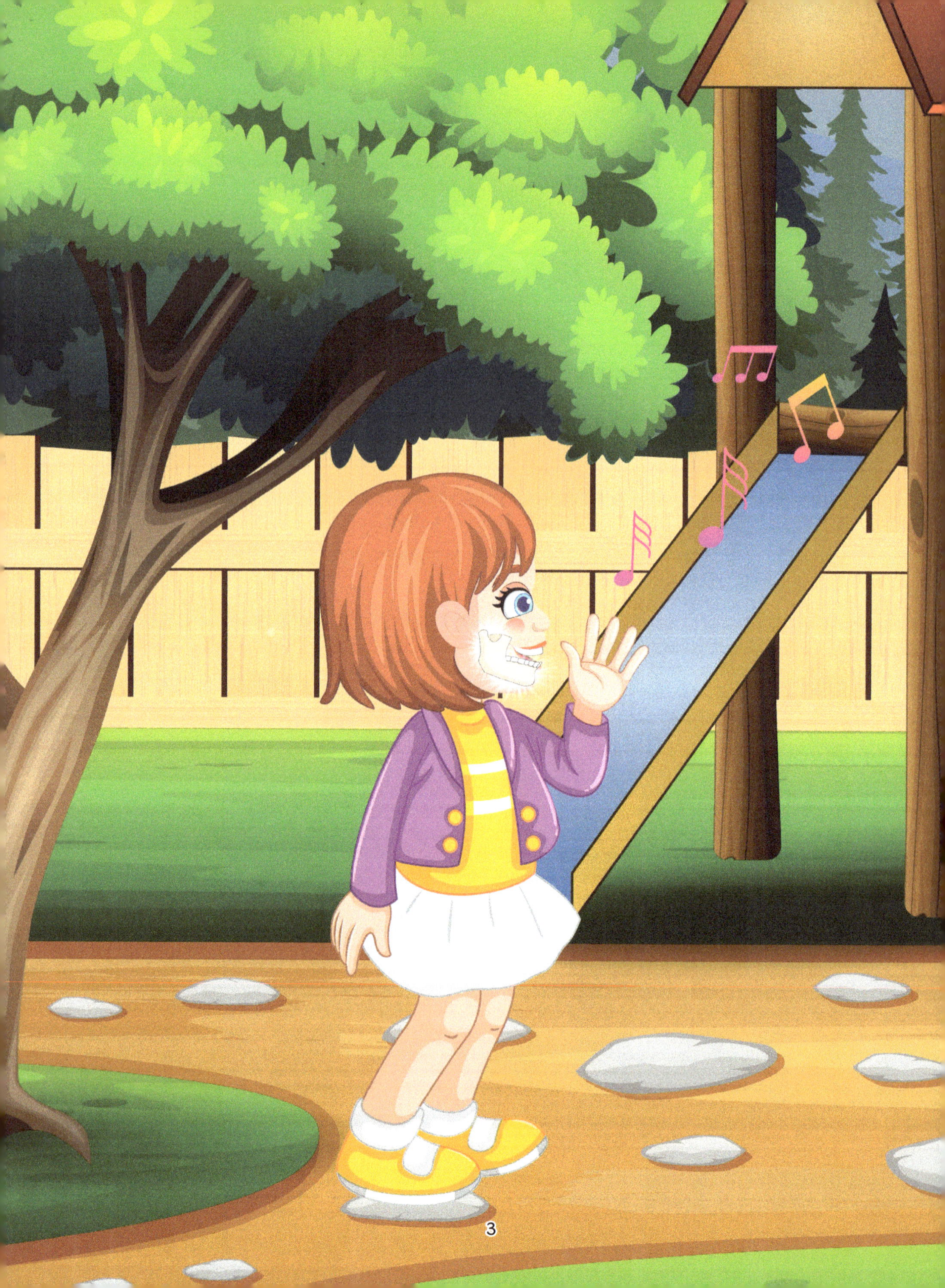

The jaw is also part of the head,
And is known as the **MANDIBLE**.

The **CLAVICLE**'s the collarbone,
And the **SCAPULA**'s the shoulder blade.

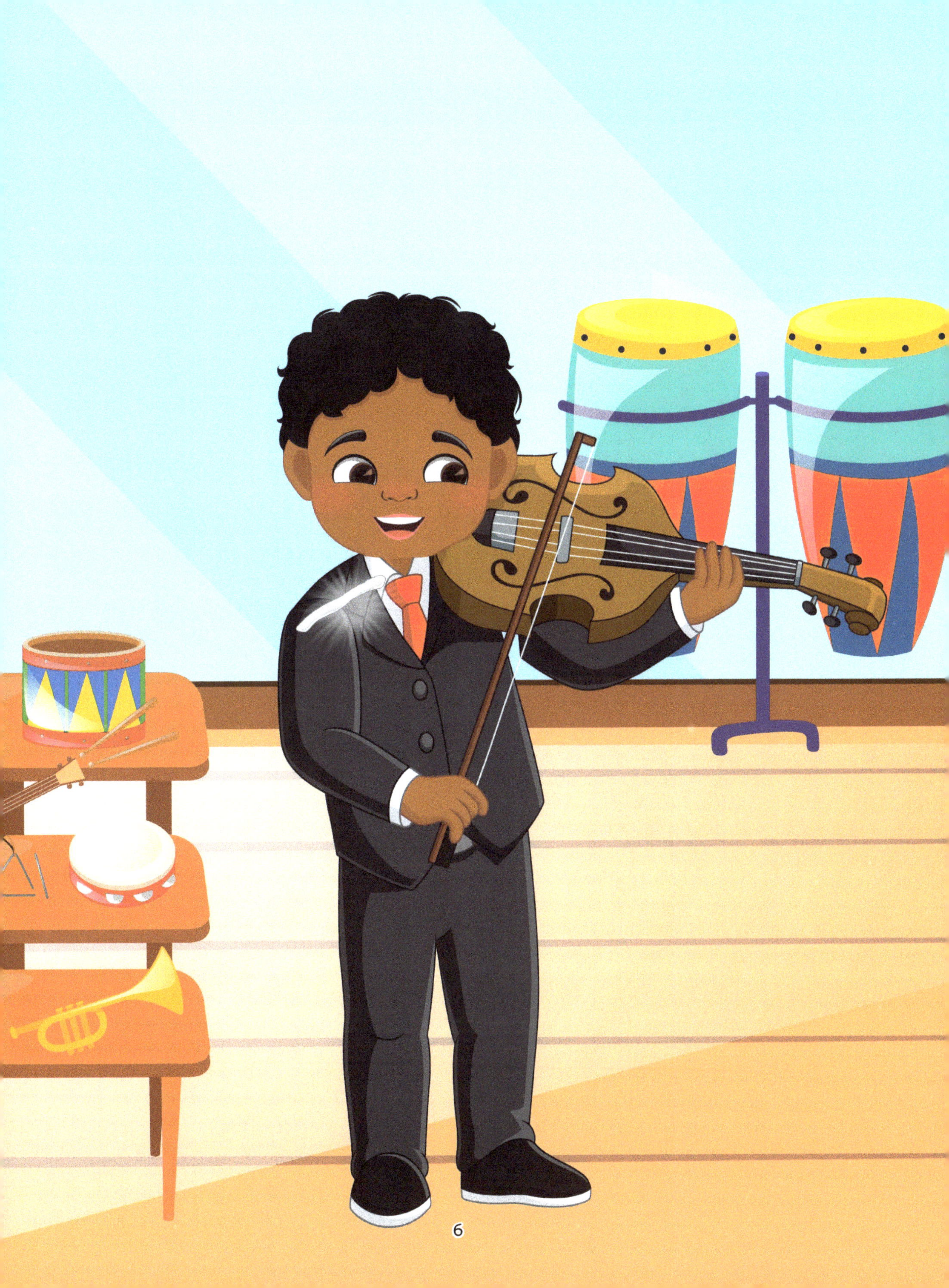

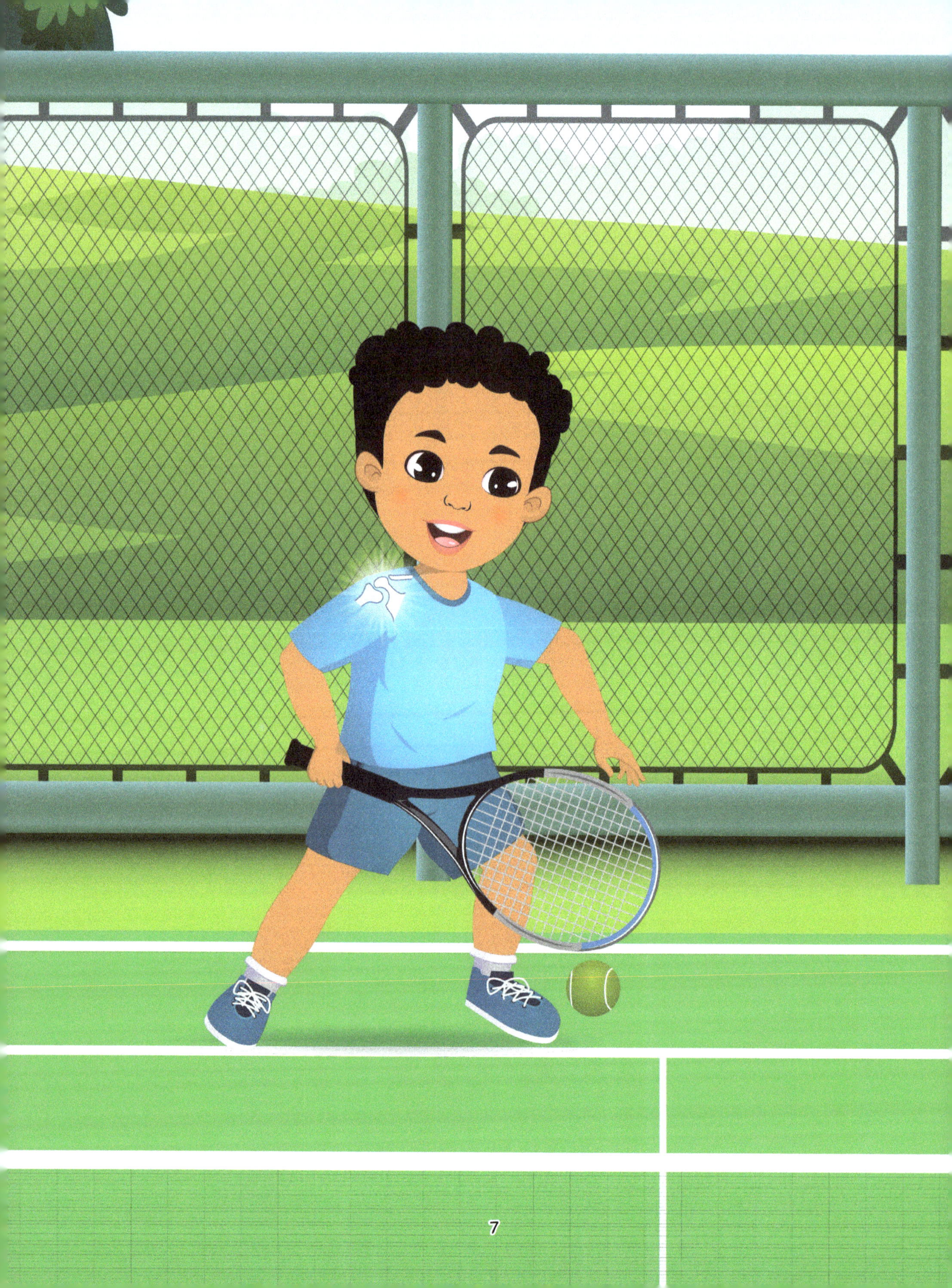

Put these together with the B & S joint,
And now the shoulders are made.

The **VERTEBRAE** start in the neck,
And hold the torso's tone.

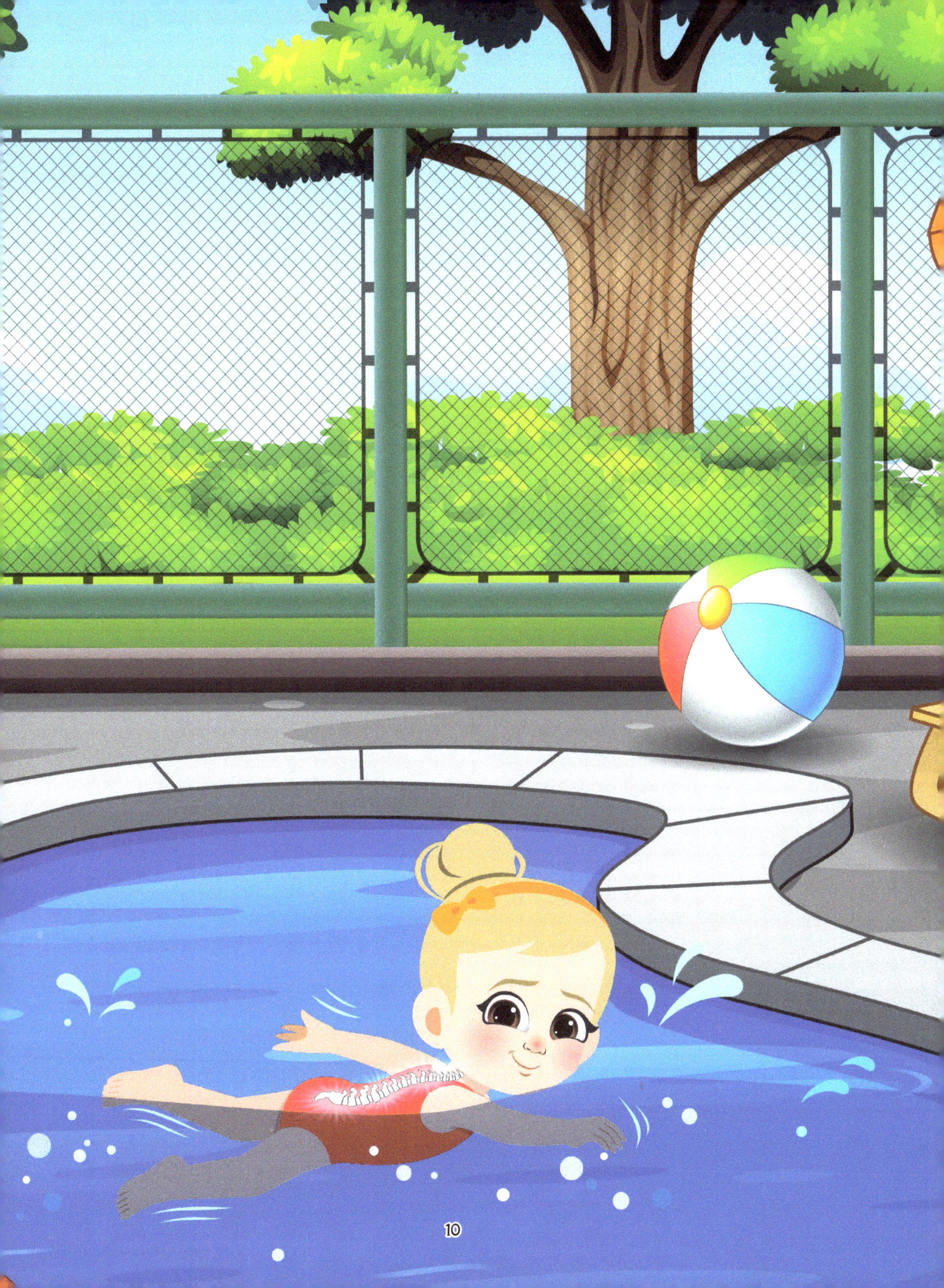

They go right through the **PELVIS** bone,
And end with the **SACRUM** bone.

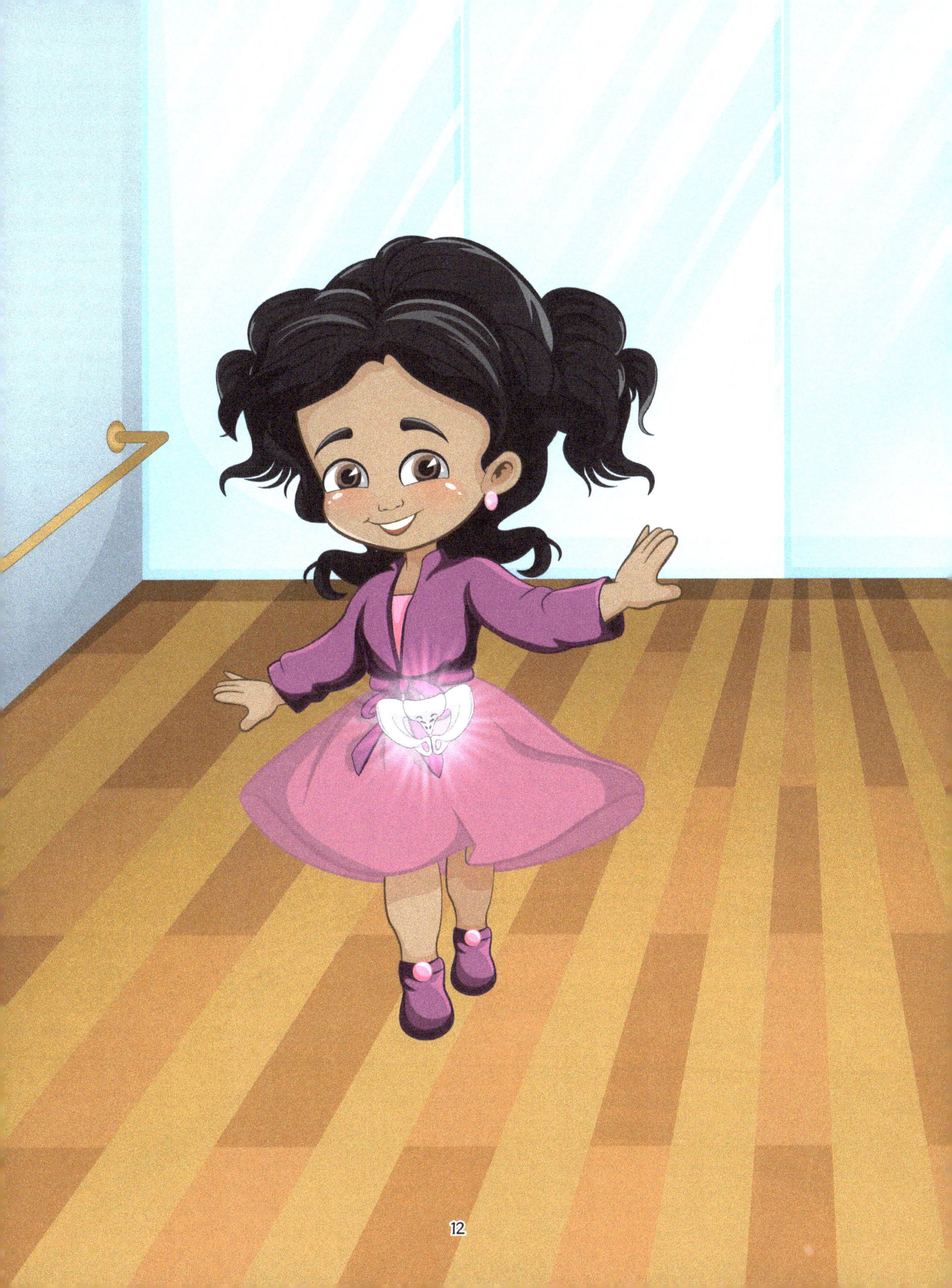

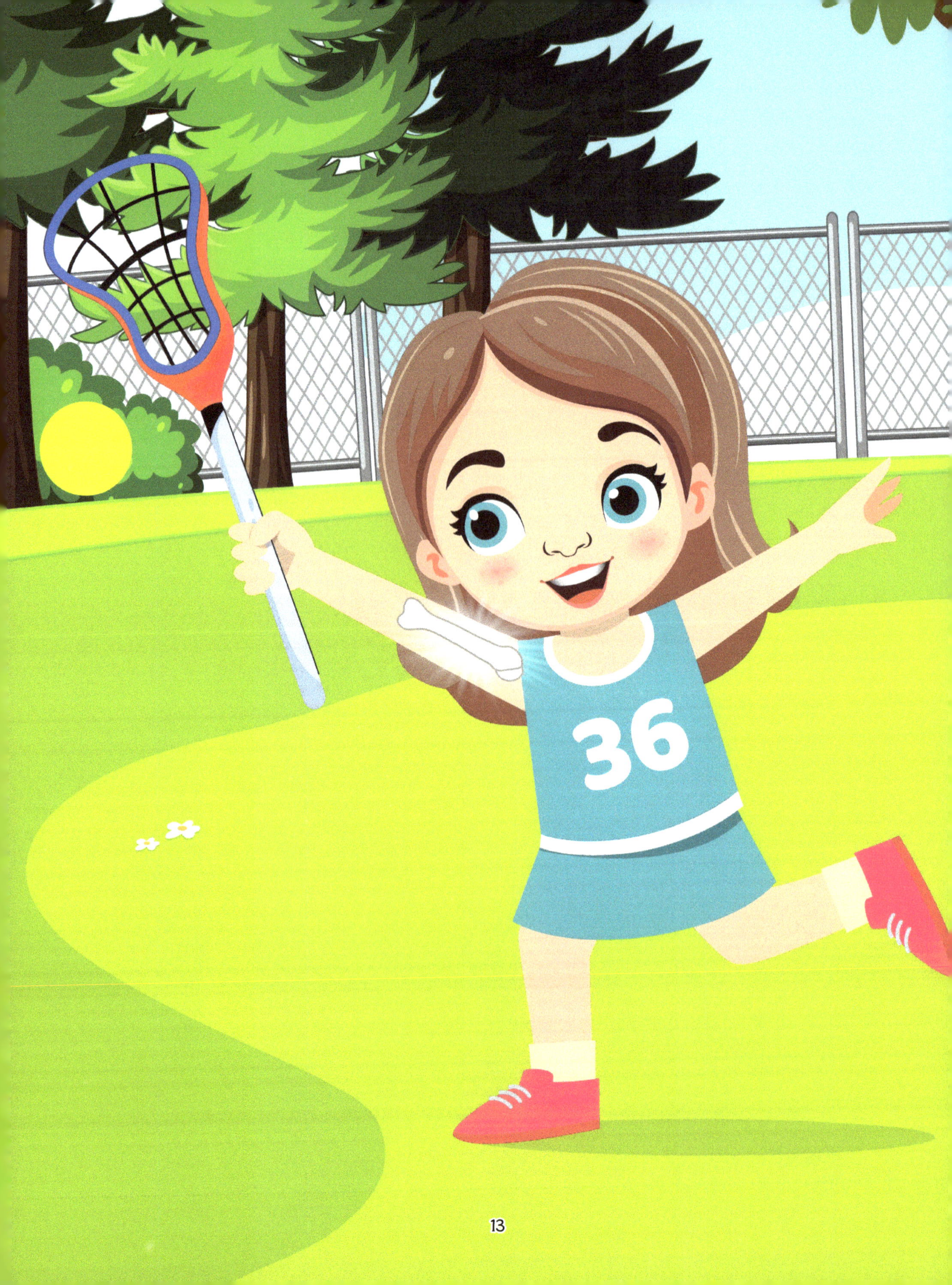
36

The upper arm just has one bone,
It's known as the **HUMERUS**.

But the lower arm is made of two,
The **ULNA** and the **RADIUS**.

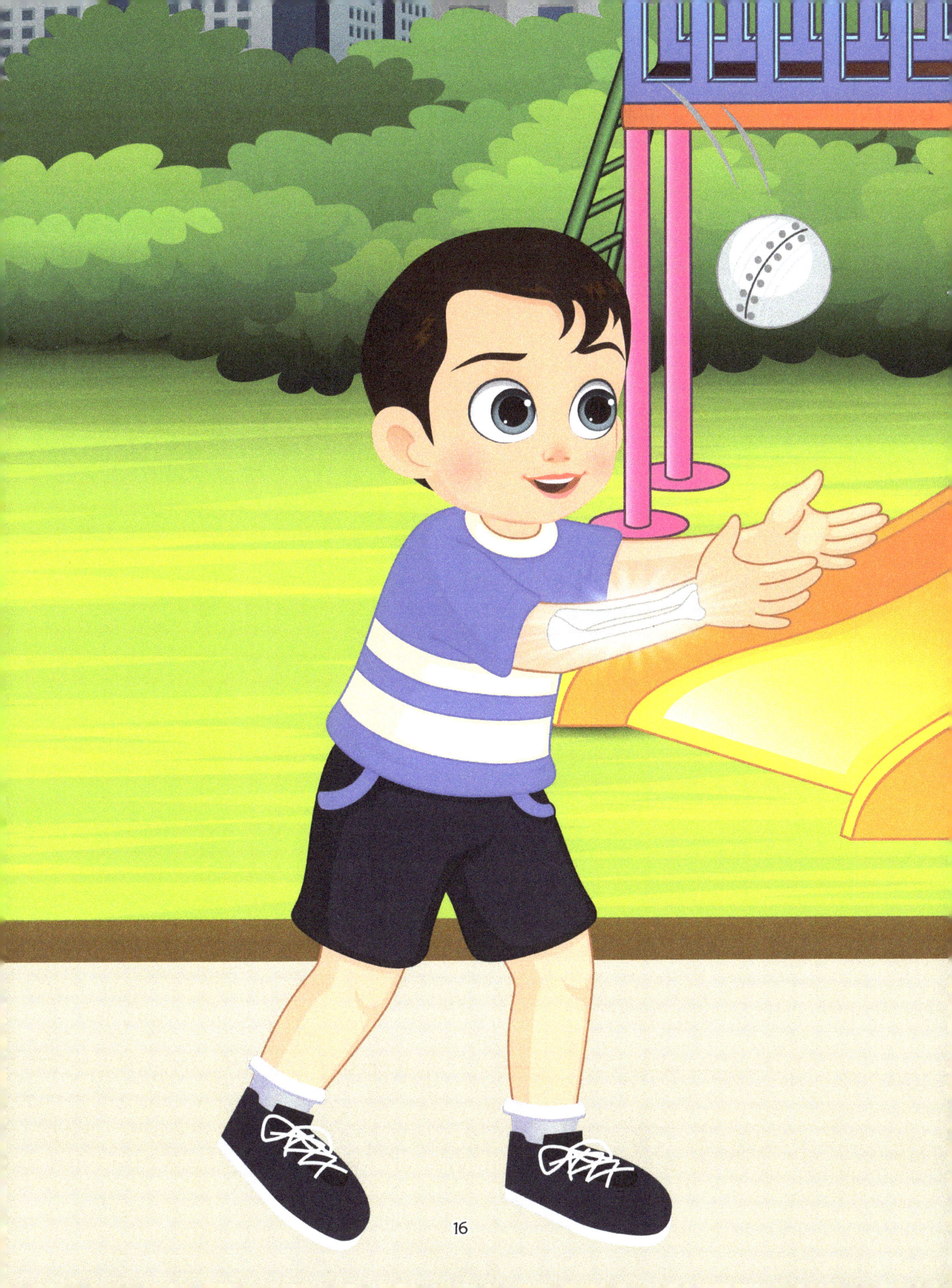

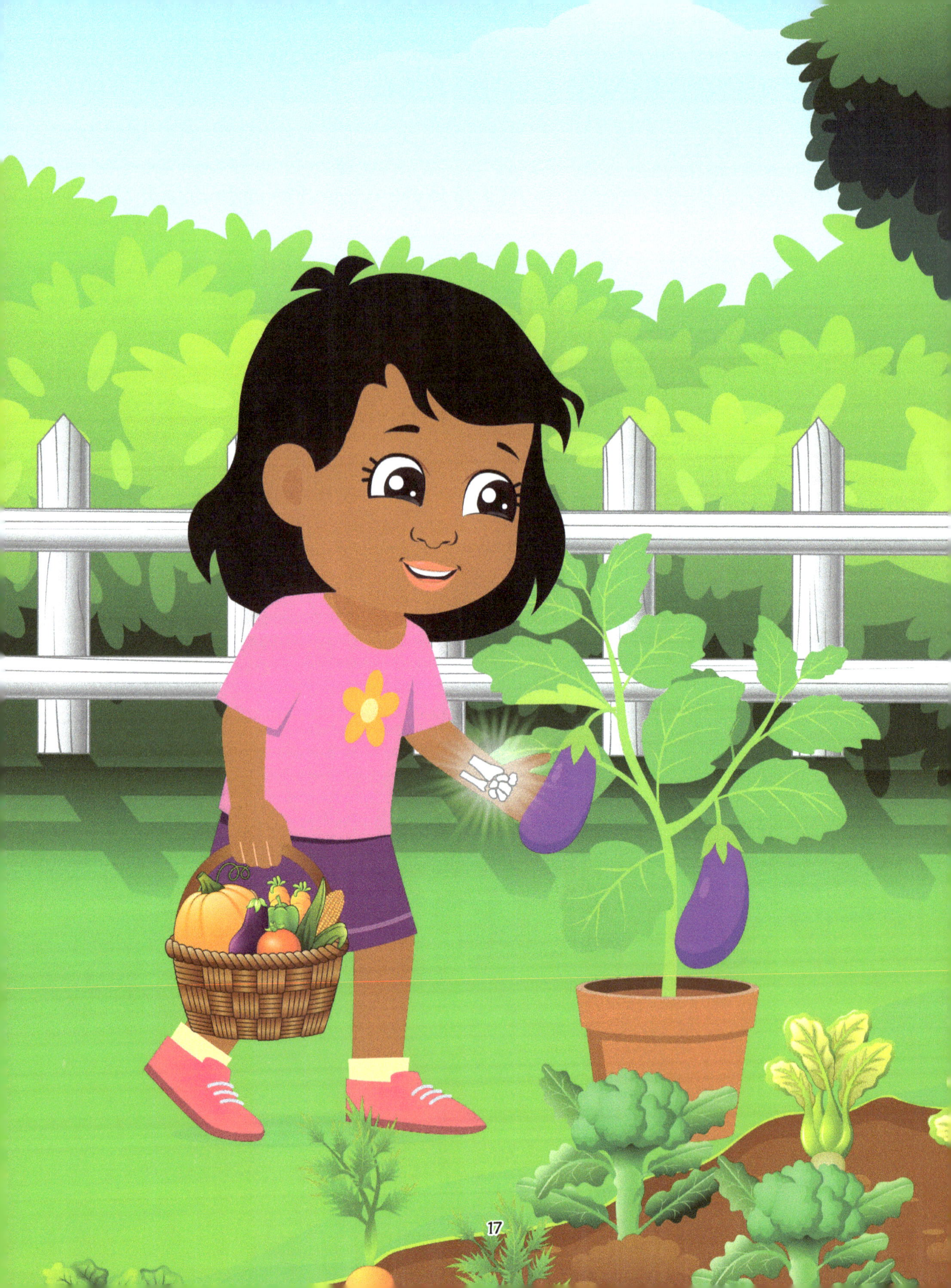

There are tons of bones in the hand,
Starting with the **CARPAL** wrist.

With **METACARPALS** and **PHALANGES** too,
They help complete a fist.

20

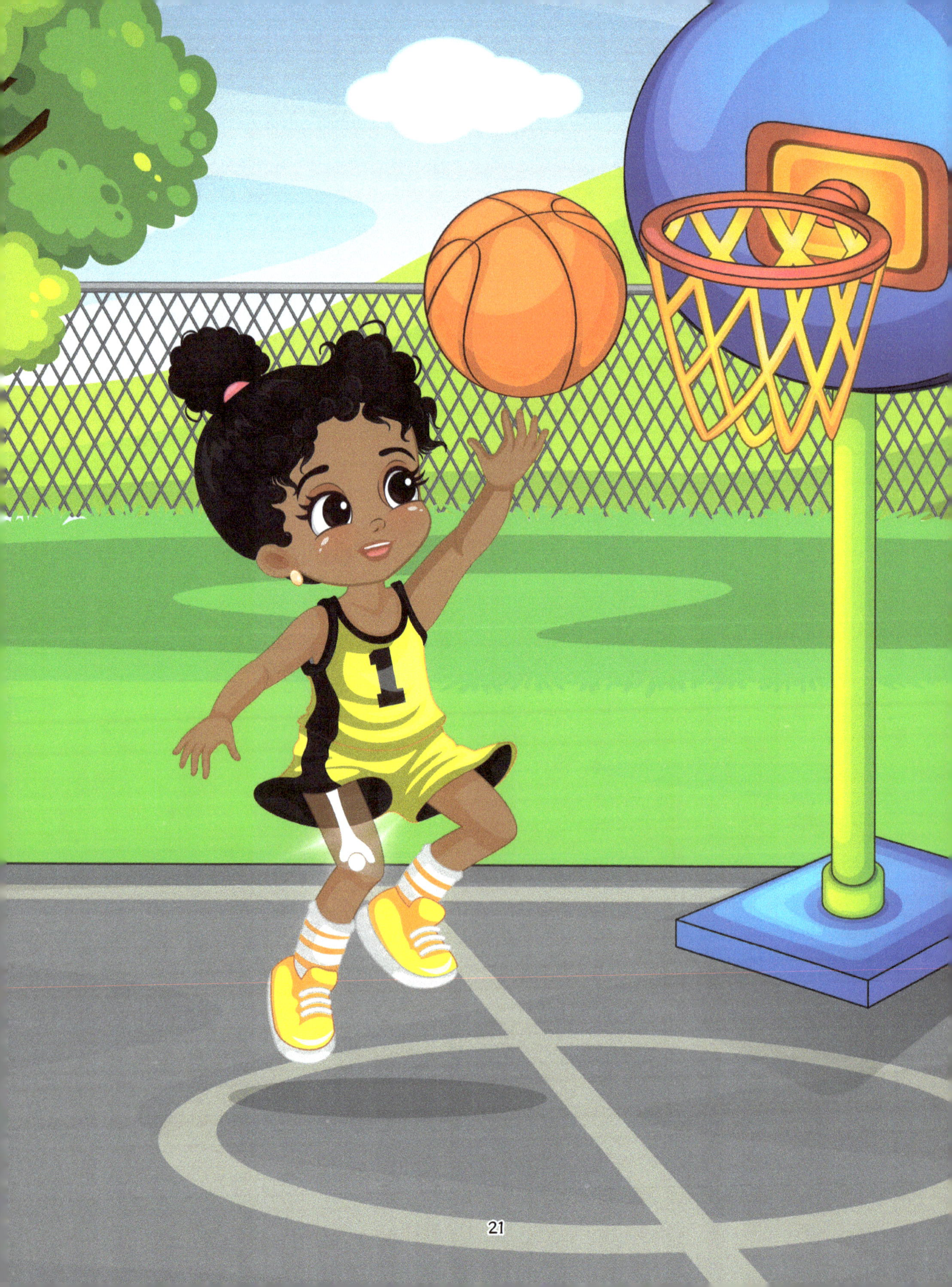

The **FEMUR** bone makes up the thigh.
The **PATELLA**'s the knee cap.

With the **TIBIA** and **FIBULA**,
The leg's made of just that!

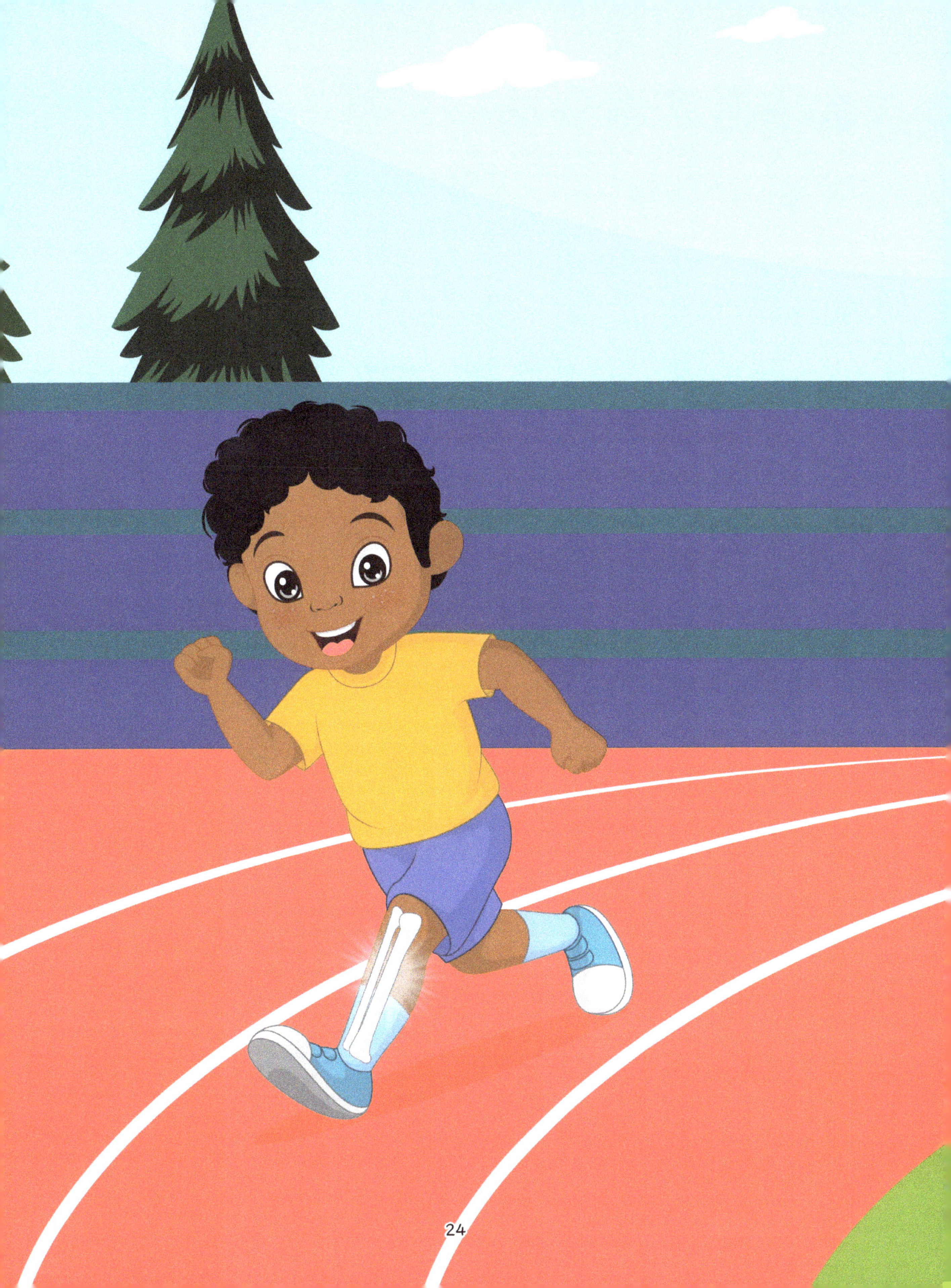

The feet are very similar,
To the hands, so it's been put.

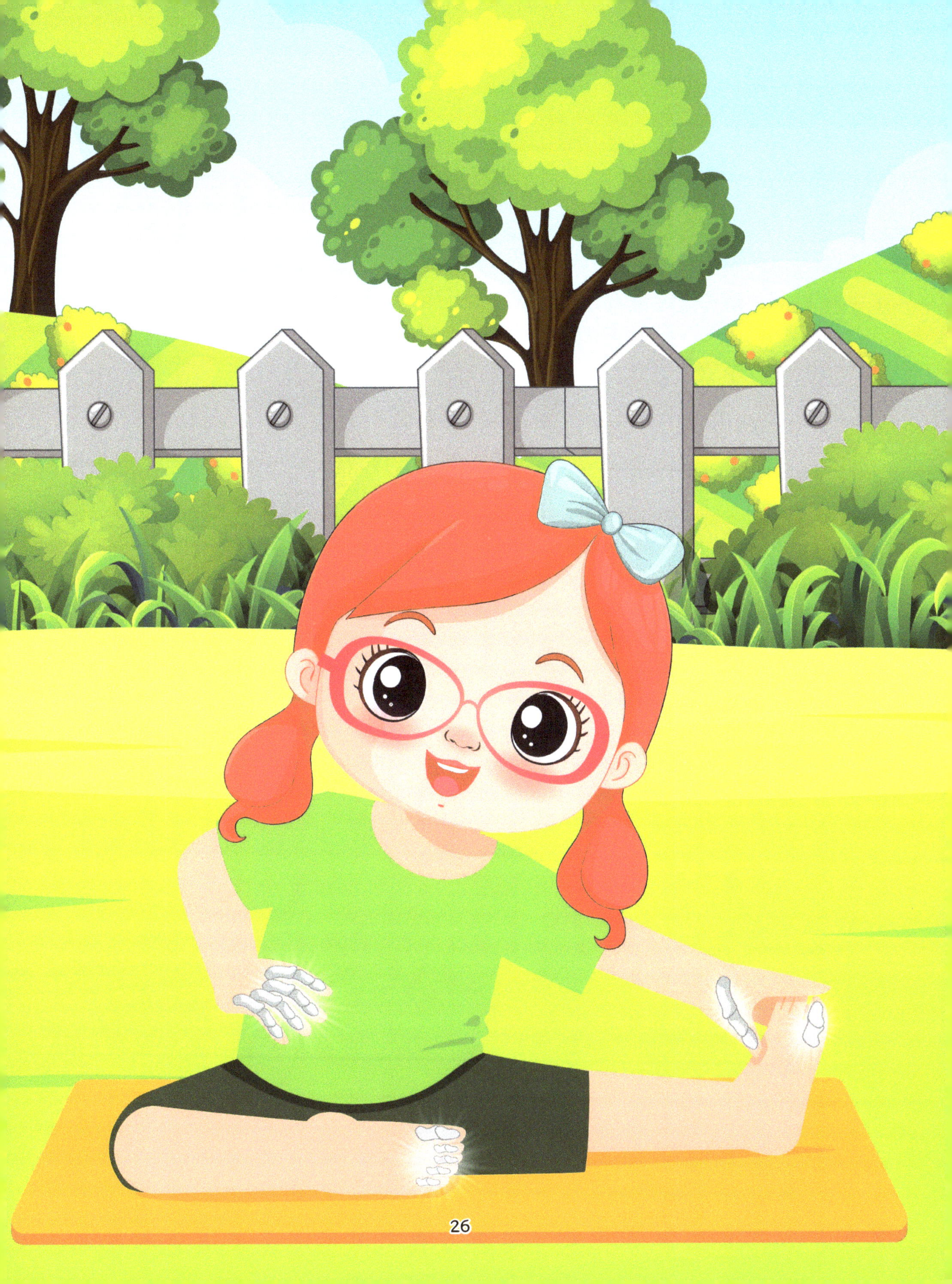

From the **TARSAL** ankle and **PHALANGE** toes, to the **METATARSAL** foot!

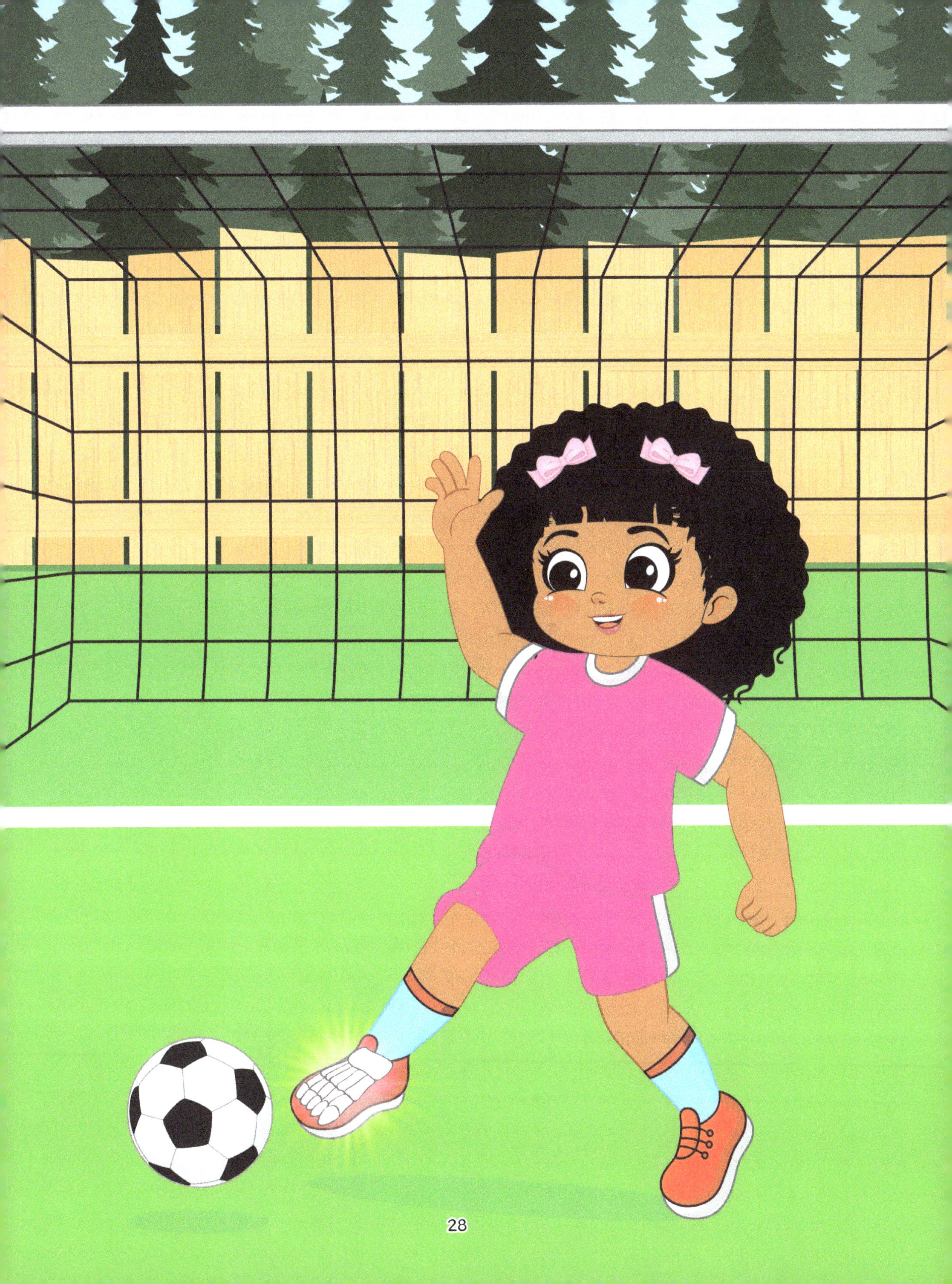

The Joints Jingle

Read along or sing to the tune of "Oh My Darlin'"

There are fixed joints.
There are hinged joints.
There are ball-and-sockets too.
These are just a couple different,
Things that help to make you, you!
The skull is fixed,
But not the fingers,
'Cause they are hinged right to the tips.
The ball and sockets form the shoulders,
And they also form the hips.

Although we all look different on the outside, we are all built the same on the inside. Let's celebrate our differences because the world would not be nearly as beautiful if everyone looked the exact same. The individuality and uniqueness of our world add color, beauty and life. Embrace it, own it and celebrate it.

Author's Note

As a teacher, I have often found that setting lessons to music is a simple mnemonic device that all students can use to help with memorization. Catchy tunes can help the most advanced to the most challenged students succeed in every subject. It has always been a lifelong dream of mine to get these jingles published so all people would be able to use them to help with their education. Keep an eye out for my other educational jingles!

Printed in the USA
CPSIA information can be obtained
at www.ICGtesting.com
LVHW060101150524
779592LV00003B/102